Watch It Grow

Life Cycles

Siân Smith

www.heinemannraintree.com
Visit our website to find out
more information about
Heinemann-Raintree books.

To order:

☎ Phone 888-454-2279

💻 Visit www.heinemannraintree.com
to browse our catalog and order online.

© 2012 Heinemann Library
an imprint of Capstone Global Library, LLC
Chicago, Illinois

Customer Service: 888-454-2279
Visit our website at www.heinemannraintree.com

Edited by Rebecca Rissman, Daniel Nunn, and Harriet Milles
Designed by Joanna Hinton-Malivoire
Picture research by Mica Brancic
Originated by Capstone Global Library Ltd.
Production by Eirian Griffiths
Printed and bound in China by Leo Paper Products Ltd

15 14 13 12 11
10 9 8 7 6 5 4 3 2 1

Library of Congress Cataloging-in-Publication Data
Smith, Siân.
  Life cycles / Sian Smith.
    p. cm.
  Includes bibliographical references and index.
  ISBN 978-1-4329-5351-5 (hc)—ISBN 978-1-4329-5496-3 (pb) 1. Life
cycles (Biology) I. Title.
  QH501.S56 2012
  571.8—dc22   2010044795

Acknowledgments
The author and publishers are grateful to the following for
permission to reproduce copyright material: Photolibrary **p.
16** (Animals Animals/Zigmund Leszczynski); Shutterstock **pp. 4
bottom left** (© Antos777), **4 bottom middle** (© Natalie Jean), **4
bottom right** (© Geanina Bechea), **4 top left** (© B. Stefanov), **4
top middle** (© Stephanie Barbary), **4 top right** (© Trucic), **5 top
left** (© Joy Brown), **5 top right** (© Outsider), **5 bottom left** (©
Alexnika), **5 bottom right** (© Natalia Yudenich), **6** (© Bluerain), **7**
(© Bogdan Wankowicz), **8** (© S-eyerkaufer), **9 left** (© Triff), **9 right**
(© Jan Zoetekouw), **10** (© Stargazer), **11 top left** (© Orionmystery@
flickr), **11 top right** (© Yellowj), **11 bottom left** (© Ann Worthy),
11 bottom right (© Eric Isselée), **12** (© Seleznev Valery), **13** (©
Koshevnyk), **14** (© Greg Henry), **15** (© Alexander Chelmodeev),
17 (© Cathy Keifer), **18** (© Petrov Anton), **19 top left** (© Splash),
19 top right (© Jan van der Hoeven), **19 bottom left** (© Torsten
Dietrich), **19 bottom right** (© Dr. Morley Read, **20 top left** (©
Melissa King), **20 top right** (© Ivan Pavlisko), **20 bottom left** (©
Privilege), **20 bottom middle & bottom right** (© Yuri Arcurs), **21
left** (© rSnapshotPhotos), **21 right** (© Monkey Business Images),
22 top left (© Marta P.), **22 top middle** (© Leolintang), **22 top
right** (© Shane W Thompson), **22 bottom left** (© Olga Lipatova),
22 bottom middle (© Pichugin Dmitry), **22 bottom right** (© Liew
Weng Keong).

Front cover photograph reproduced with permission of
Photolibrary (Stockbroker); back cover photograph Shutterstock
(© Jan Zoetekouw).

We would like to thank Michael Bright for his invaluable help in the
preparation of this book.

Every effort has been made to contact copyright holders of any
material reproduced in this book. Any omissions will be rectified in
subsequent printings if notice is given to the publisher.

Some words appear in bold, **like this.** You can find out
what they mean in "Words to Know" on page 23.

Contents

About this series

Books in this series introduce readers to the life cycle of different plants and animals. Use this book to stimulate discussion about how all living things have life cycles and how some life cycles are similar, while others are very different.

What Is a Life Cycle?

There are many different types of living things. All animals, such as birds, insects, and people are living things. All plants are living things, too. All living things have a life cycle.

A life cycle shows the changes, or different **stages**, that a living thing goes through in its life. These changes follow a **pattern**. They happen in the same order for each living thing.

Life Begins

The main **stages** in a life cycle are the same for all living things. The start of a life cycle is when life begins. An animal life cycle might start with an egg or a baby.

first leaves

shoot

seed

root

For most plants, life begins with a seed. When a seed has water and sunlight, it can begin to grow into a plant.

Growing Up

Baby animals grow up to become adults who can care for themselves. Animals and plants go through lots of different changes before they become adults.

Some living things take a long time to grow up. Others grow up quickly. A sunflower seed can become a fully grown plant in about 12 weeks. It takes an elephant many years to become an adult.

Making New Life

When animals become adults they can create new life by making babies. This is called **reproduction**. Plants make new plants by reproducing, too.

ladybug **larva**

Some animals start life inside their mother's body. Some animals start life in eggs. Some baby animals look very different from their parents at first. Others look just like their parents.

pollen

Most plants make new life with seeds. To make a seed, **pollen** has to get from one part of a flower to another. Pollen can be carried by the wind, or by insects, birds, and bats.

seed

Once a flower has the pollen it needs, a seed starts to grow inside the flower. Seeds have cases around them to keep them safe. Inside each seed is the start of a new plant.

Dying

Nothing that is living can stay alive forever. After time, all living things will get old and die. This is part of the life cycle, too.

young tree

Dying is the last **stage** in a life cycle. But life cycles go on because animals make babies and plants make seeds. This starts the life cycle all over again.

Unusual Life Cycles

old skin

Many animals go through amazing changes to become adults. Some animals grow new skin. They lose their old skin as they grow up. This is called **molting**.

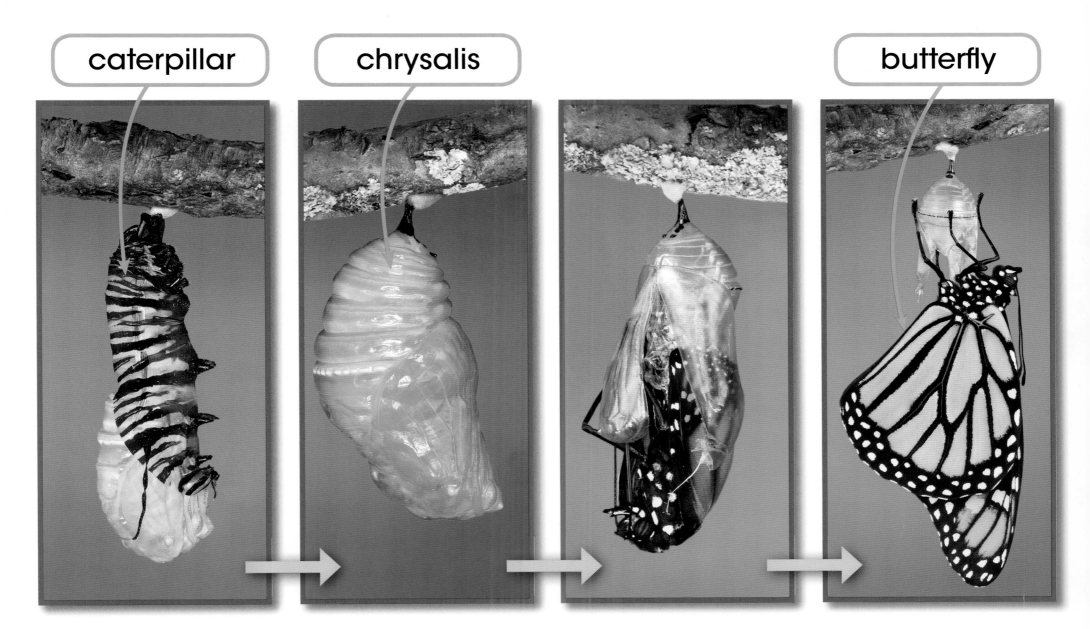

caterpillar

chrysalis

butterfly

Some insects change completely when they turn into adults. A butterfly starts life as a caterpillar. It spins a cover around its body, called a **chrysalis**. Inside the chrysalis it changes into an adult!

17

frog

Another special group of animals are called **amphibians**. Amphibians are animals such as frogs, toads, and newts. They are born in water, but they spend most of their lives on land.

18

Amphibians lay their eggs in water. The young have **gills** so they can breathe underwater, and tails to help them swim. As they grow, they get **lungs** to breathe in air, and legs for moving on land.

The Human Life Cycle

Humans have life cycles, too. A baby becomes a child. A child becomes a teenager, and then an adult. Adults get older, and eventually they die. When adults have babies, they start the life cycle all over again.

As we grow, our bodies do not change on the outside as much as butterflies or frogs do. Humans take care of their young and teach them new things for much longer than other animals.

How Long Is One Life Cycle?

olive tree

human

sea lion

marigold

hippopotamus

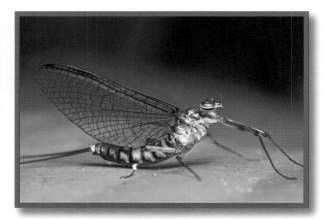

mayfly

How long do you think the living things in the photos might live for?

Answers on page 23

Words to Know

amphibian type of animal that can live in water or on land

chrysalis case around an insect. Inside a chrysalis, an insect changes into an adult.

gills part of an animal's body that helps it to breathe underwater

larva young insect

lung part of an animal's body that helps it to breathe in air

molting growing new skin and losing the old skin

pattern happening in the same order

pollen powder made by plants. Plants reproduce by using pollen.

reproduction to make new life

stage one part or section of a life cycle

Answers to quiz on page 22:
olive tree about 500 to 900 years
human about 70 to 80 years
sea lion about 17 years
marigold about 1 year
hippopotamus about 45 years
mayfly about 30 minutes to 1 day

Index

Note to Parents and Teachers

Before reading

Show the children the front cover of the book. Ask them what they think life cycle means. Explain to the children that a life cycle shows the changes or different stages a living thing goes through in its life.

After reading

- Depending on the time of year, ask each child to create a book about a living thing's life cycle. For example, if it is fall, ask them to make a story about the life cycle of an apple tree. Each page can show one stage of the living thing's life cycle.
- Cut out pictures of different stages of a life cycle. Ask children to order and name the stages. Stick the pictures or photos in the correct order on a display chart.
- As an ongoing class activity, plant a fast-growing seed of a plant that also produces seeds quickly (for example, a bean). Encourage the children to observe the changes and stages of its life cycle week by week.